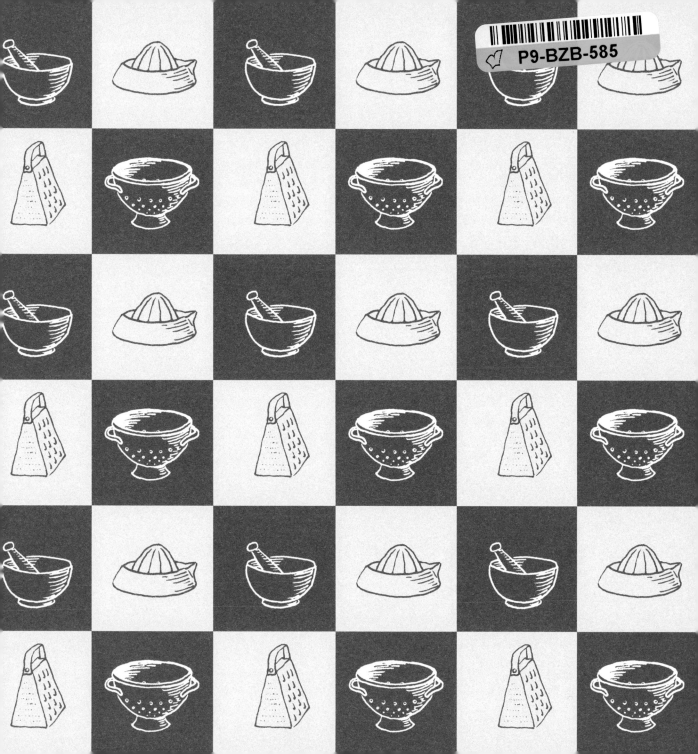

CHOCOLATE

CHOCOLATE
A Book of Recipes

LORENZ BOOKS
NEW YORK • LONDON • SYDNEY • BATH

This edition published in 1996 by Lorenz Books
an imprint of Anness Publishing Limited
administrative office: 27 West 20th Street
New York, NY 10011

Lorenz Books are available for bulk purchase for sales promotion and for
premium use. For details write or call the Manager of Special Sales,
Lorenz Books, 27 West 20th Street, New York, NY 10011; (212) 807-6739.

Produced by Anness Publishing Limited
1 Boundary Row
London SE1 8HP

ISBN 1 85967 232 9

Publisher Joanna Lorenz
Senior Cookery Editor Linda Fraser
Cookery Editor Anne Hildyard
Designer Lisa Tai
Illustrations Anna Koska
Photographers Karl Adamson, Edward Allwright, Steve Baxter, James Duncan, Amanda Heywood and Don Last
Recipes Catherine Atkinson, Alex Barker, Elizabeth Wolf-Cohen, Frances Cleary, Christine France,
Sarah Gates, Shirley Gill, Patricia Lousada and Norma MacMillan
Food for photography Carla Capalbo, Elizabeth Wolf-Cohen, Frances Cleary, Carole Handslip,
Wendy Lee and Jane Stevenson
Stylists Madeleine Brehaut, Maria Kelly, Blake Minton and Fiona Tillett
Jacket photography Amanda Heywood

Typeset by MC Typeset Ltd, Rochester, Kent
Printed in Singapore by
Star Standard Industries Pte Ltd

Contents

$\mathcal{I}$NTRODUCTION

Wicked, decadent, rich, mouth-watering, "to die for". Guess which one ingredient crops up in the dishes described? If you need some more clues, try "a chocoholic's delight" or "a chocolate lover's dream come true". Yes, it's chocolate, one of the most emotive of ingredients; and certainly one of the most popular.

But the chocolate which we know and love nowadays has not always been consumed in this form. When Cortés and his conquistadors were treated to a banquet by the Aztec emperor Montezuma in 1519, they were given cold chocolate to drink in sumptuous gold goblets. This rather bitter, spicy drink was completely different from our hot drinking chocolate. It was thickened by maize and flavoured with vanilla and ginger and often chilli and turmeric. Nowadays breakfast in Mexico is likely to be washed down with a drink of sweetened hot chocolate flavoured with spices such as cinnamon and ginger. The word itself is derived from *xocolatl*, the Aztec word for their cocoa-based drink.

The trade with Europe began to develop during the latter part of the 16th century, as a result of the Spanish conquests in Mexico and Central America. During the 17th century, chocolate houses became extremely fashionable among the wealthy in large cities such as Florence, Brussels, Vienna and London.

The drink was, however, no longer a cold, bitter drink but a hot, sweetened drink. It was not until the mid 1800's that chocolate lost some of its exclusive tag and became available to the masses. This followed Van Houten's invention, in his native Holland in 1828, of a machine to extract the cocoa butter from the bean. There was a surge of interest in Britain, advanced by the famous Quaker families, the Frys, Rowntrees, Terrys and Cadburys. Their primary aim was to promote drinking chocolate as a healthier alternative to gin! But when Joseph Fry discovered, in 1847, that by adding chocolate liquor and sugar to cocoa butter, a solid, eating chocolate was formed, the chocolate bar was born. Understandably, it did not take long for chocolate in the form of food, rather than drink, to catch on.

And it has caught on, all over the world.

In this delectable book, you will find chocolate blending with such different ingredients as chestnuts, dates, blueberries, apricots and brandy. One of the most versatile of sweet ingredients, whether it is dark, milk or white chocolate, it serves to give pleasure and has come to signify sharing and love. It is one of the most-prized of foods. Little wonder the Aztecs called it "food of the gods".

Sue Lawrence

TYPES OF CHOCOLATE

COCOA POWDER

The residue left after the cocoa butter has been pressed from the ground, roasted beans. Sweetened cocoa is used for drinks. In the U.S., this is blended with milk powder and used to make "hot chocolate". Unsweetened cocoa powder is used for baking.

TYPES OF BLOCK CHOCOLATE

The quality of block chocolate varies according to the quantity of cocoa butter it contains. Most types have around 27 per cent. The higher the proportion of cocoa butter, the more easily the chocolate melts.

MILK CHOCOLATE

Rarely used for cooking, this chocolate tastes good because of added sugar and condensed or powdered milk.

BITTERSWEET, SEMISWEET OR SWEET CHOCOLATE

A pleasant-tasting chocolate because it contains some sugar, it is often used for cooking. The amount of added sugar determines its name.

UNSWEETENED OR BITTER CHOCOLATE

Unsweetened with a high proportion of cocoa butter, this is used mainly for baking.

WHITE CHOCOLATE

This is creamy in color and texture as it does not contain any cocoa solids but does contain cocoa butter and sugar. It does not set quite as firmly as milk and dark chocolate.

COUVERTURE CHOCOLATE

Used by professional cooks because it melts smoothly, it has a high cocoa butter content (up to 50 per cent) but needs tempering. Couverture chocolate comes in semisweet, bittersweet, milk and white options.

CHOCOLATE CHIPS AND SPRINKLES

Chips are added to cookies and cakes, and sprinkles are scattered over frosted cakes.

ORGANIC CHOCOLATE

This is made without chemical additives.

Cocoa powder

Organic chocolate

White couverture chocolate

Semisweet chocolate
chips

Milk couverture chocolate

Semisweet chocolate curls

White chocolate
curls

White chocolate

Milk chocolate

Chocolate sprinkles

Semisweet chocolate

Bittersweet couverture chocolate

White chocolate
chips

White chocolate chips

Milk chocolate chips

$\mathcal{B}$ASIC $\mathcal{T}$ECHNIQUES

When melting chocolate for use in recipes, all equipment must be completely dry. Do not cover during or after melting because any water or condensation could cause the chocolate to seize or stiffen.

Of the methods shown below, the double boiler method is the most traditional and reliable. The direct heat method is a little more tricky and best used when another ingredient such as cream, milk or butter is added.

Melting by microwaving is fast but must be checked at 5–10-second intervals as the chocolate could quite easily burn.

Fill half of the lower part of the double boiler with water and bring it to simmering point. Place the chopped or broken chocolate in the top part. With the heat low, melt the chocolate slowly, stirring to distribute the heat evenly. Remove the bowl as soon as the chocolate is fully melted. If you do not have a double boiler, place a small heatproof bowl over a saucepan so that it sits above the water, and melt the chocolate as above.

Place the chocolate with the milk, cream or butter in a heavy-bottomed saucepan and melt over a low heat, stirring constantly. Do not leave the chocolate unattended and take it off the heat as soon as it is smooth.

For 4 ounces dark or semisweet chocolate, place the broken-up chocolate in a microwave-safe bowl and microwave on medium power (50 per cent) for about 2 minutes. For the same amount of milk or white chocolate, melt on low power (30 per cent) for about 2 minutes. These are approximate times based on a 650–700 watt oven. Ovens vary so check the chocolate halfway through – it will look shiny but still in shape.

TEMPERING CHOCOLATE

When using couverture chocolate or if preparing to make molded chocolates, coatings or sophisticated decorations, it must be tempered for good results. This is a procedure where the chocolate is gently heated and cooled to stabilize the cocoa solids and butter which would otherwise cause cooked chocolate to "bloom" – become cloudy or dull in appearance. Tempering makes the chocolate very shiny and easy to work. Chocolate for general baking does not require tempering.

1 Melt the couverture chocolate until it has reached a temperature of 110°F. Stir well until it is melted and smooth.

2 Pour out three-quarters on to a marble slab. Using a spatula, scrape into a pool and spread out again. Work for 3–5 minutes then mix with the remaining chocolate. Reheat to 85°F before use.

COATING OR DIPPING

For recipes that require coating or dipping such as candies, truffles, caramels, dried and fresh fruit and cookies, use tempered couverture chocolate for the best results. If this is hard to find, melt bittersweet or semisweet chocolate but chill immediately to avoid a bloom forming on the surface.

Melt the chocolate then pour it into a bowl for dipping. The temperature should be about 115°F. Use a skewer or fondue fork to lower the sweet or fruit into the chocolate. Turn to coat and lift out, tapping to remove excess. Place the dipped candy or fruit on a nonstick baking sheet until dry. Chill immediately.

11

$\mathcal{D}$ECORATING WITH $\mathcal{C}$HOCOLATE

QUICK CHOCOLATE CURLS

These are used as a simple decoration on a variety of cakes and desserts. For best effect, make a large amount and pile them on in an elegant profusion. Easy to make, they can be stored for weeks in an airtight container.

1 Bring a bar of chocolate to room temperature. Using a vegetable peeler with a swivel blade, peel the edge of the chocolate bar towards you, making small curls. Let them fall on to a sheet of wax paper.

2 Use a skewer or toothpick to transfer the curls on to the dessert singly, or use a cool knife to slide a whole line of curls. Do not touch the curls with fingers as they will melt easily.

CHUNKY CHOCOLATE CURLS

These add a professional look to desserts and cakes, yet are fairly easy to make with a swivel-bladed peeler. Work quickly or the chocolate will have to be reheated.

1 Using tempered chocolate, pour it into a pan lined with baking parchment, to produce a block about 1-inch thick. Chill until set.

2 Allow to come to room temperature, remove the chocolate block from the pan, then use a swivel-bladed peeler to make short chunky curls.

MAKING CHOCOLATE SHAPES

Chocolate shapes add an attractive finish to mousses and cakes. The simplest of all shapes to make is the triangle. You can also make squares or semi-circles using pastry cutters, or any decorative shape such as hearts or stars with small metal cookie cutters.

Use melted and tempered couverture chocolate for shiny and long-lasting results, but if this is not available, ordinary melted good quality dark or cooking chocolate is fine.

1 Pour melted chocolate onto a marble slab. Spread evenly with a spatula. Cool until firm.

2 With a sharp knife cut the chocolate into a rectangle, then cut into small squares and then triangles. Alternatively, use cutters to stamp out decorative shapes.

CHOCOLATE LEAVES

Making chocolate leaves requires a delicate touch but they are worth the effort because they enhance any dessert or cake they decorate. Use fresh and non-toxic leaves that have good veins such as rose, bay or lemon leaves.

1 Wash and dry the leaves thoroughly before use. Melt the chocolate and with a pastry brush or spoon, coat the veined side of each leaf. Be careful not to get chocolate on the other side or it will be difficult to remove.

2 Place the coated leaves with the chocolate side up on a sheet of baking parchment and leave to set.

With cool hands, peel back the leaf from the stem end. If not used immediately, store them in a cool place.

$\mathcal{U}$SING $\mathcal{C}$HOCOLATE

CHOCOLATE CUPS

These simple, chocolate cups can be used as an elegant dessert or *petits fours* when filled with mousse, ice cream or chocolate ganache. Use small or medium paper cup liners that are usually available from specialty kitchen stores.

1 Melt the chocolate and, with a pastry brush, coat the inside of the cases with a layer of chocolate. Allow this to set. Repeat with a second layer. Leave to set.

2 With cool hands, carefully peel off the paper cases. They can be filled as required. Keep the chocolate cups cold until ready to serve.

SPICED MOCHA DRINK   Serves 4

A rich and warming drink that is not for weight watchers but tastes absolutely heavenly.

Chop or grate 6 ounces of semisweet or milk chocolate. Melt it in a double boiler with ½ cup of light cream, stirring well. When the mixture is blended, remove from the heat. Making sure the coffee and the chocolate are at the same temperature, stir in 3 cups of hot black coffee and ¼ teaspoon of ground cinnamon. Beat with a small whisk until frothy. Serve it hot in tall glasses or mugs topped with a scoop of whipped cream. As an optional decoration, sprinkle with cocoa powder.

CULINARY USES

Chocolate has a reputation for being both an aphrodisiac and an energizer (it contains caffeine) but it is said to be addictive and a source of migraine. Despite this, however, chocolate is very popular and is used in cooking in many ways: in drinks, desserts, candies, cakes, pastries, ganache, ice creams and sauces, often in combination with other flavors such as vanilla, cinnamon, nuts, coffee and orange. Chocolate is also found in some unusual dishes, such as Italian chocolate-flavored pasta, served as a dessert, and the Mexican dish of *mole* – turkey, chilies and semisweet chocolate.

BUYING AND STORING

Always buy the best quality chocolate for cooking as this will give a smoother, richer result. The best chocolate has a higher cocoa butter content, for example couverture chocolate (with up to 50 per cent cocoa butter), which is used by professional bakers and confectioners but must be tempered before use. Store chocolate in a dry, cool place away from sunlight and well wrapped to prevent it from absorbing any other flavors. Store away from strong odors. Bittersweet, semisweet or sweet chocolate will keep for up to a year in dry, cool conditions. Milk chocolate can be kept for up to six months.

TIPS AND HINTS

• Chocolate must be melted very slowly as it can easily become overcooked and refuse to hold together.

• When melting chocolate, care must be taken not to let any water into it or it may stiffen and become totally unworkable. If it does, correct this by stirring in one teaspoon at a time of fat such as cocoa butter, vegetable oil, vegetable shortening or clarified unsalted 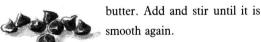 butter. Add and stir until it is smooth again.

• Chocolate that has developed a bloom in a fridge can still be melted and used in recipes but it is unsuitable for grating or making curls.

• If adding liquid to melted chocolate, make sure that they are both at the same temperature. If the chocolate is hotter than the liquid, the chocolate may become lumpy; if it is colder, the cocoa butter may separate out.

• When chopping or grating chocolate, a dry board, knife and grater must be used. Chill the chocolate before beginning and, on a warm day, it is a good idea if the utensils are also chilled first. You can use a food processor but care must be taken not to over-process as it may become sticky and clump together.

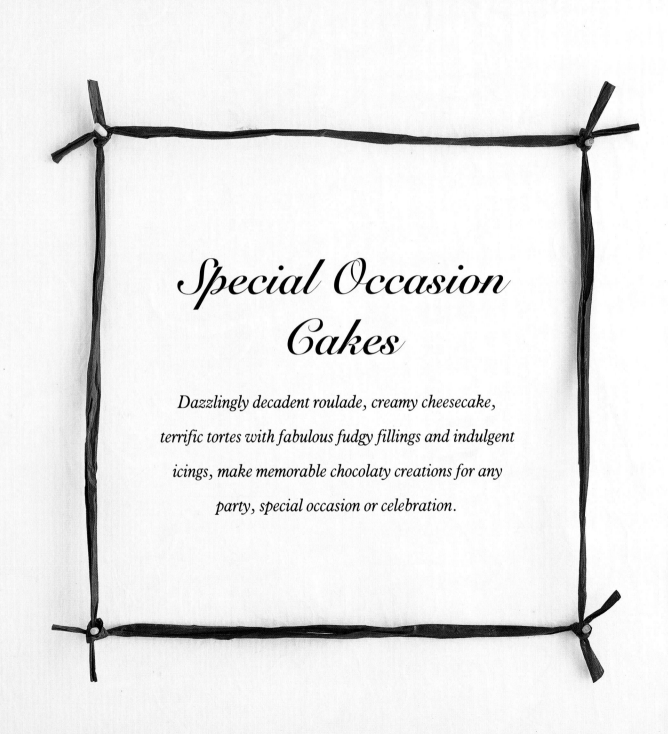

Special Occasion Cakes

Dazzlingly decadent roulade, creamy cheesecake, terrific tortes with fabulous fudgy fillings and indulgent icings, make memorable chocolaty creations for any party, special occasion or celebration.

CHOCOLATE DATE TORTE

A stunning cake that tastes wonderful. Rich and gooey – it's a chocoholic's delight!

Serves 8

scant 1 cup sour cream

scant 1 cup mascarpone

1 teaspoon vanilla extract, plus a few
*   extra drops*

confectioner's sugar, to taste

4 egg whites

1/2 cup superfine sugar

7 ounces semisweet chocolate

scant 1 cup Medjool dates, pitted
*   and chopped*

1 1/2 cups walnuts or pecans, chopped

Preheat the oven to 350°F. Lightly grease and base-line an 8-inch spring-form cake pan. For the frosting, mix together the sour cream and mascarpone, and add a few drops of vanilla extract and confectioner's sugar to taste. Set aside. Whisk the egg whites in a bowl until they peak stiffly. Whisk in 2 tablespoons of the superfine sugar until thick and glossy, then fold in the rest. Chop 6 ounces of the chocolate. Carefully fold into the meringue with the dates, nuts, and 1 teaspoon of the vanilla extract. Pour into the pan, spread level and bake for 45 minutes, until risen. Cool in the pan for 10 minutes, then turn out on to a wire rack. Peel off the lining paper and leave until cold. Frost over the top of the torte. Melt the remaining chocolate in a bowl over hot water. Spoon into a paper icing bag, snip off the top and drizzle the chocolate over the torte. Chill before serving.

FRENCH CHOCOLATE CAKE

This is typical of a French homemade cake – dense, dark, and delicious. The texture is very different from a sponge cake and it is excellent served with cream or a fruit coulis.

Serves 10–12

generous 1/2 cup superfine sugar, plus extra for sprinkling

10 ounces semisweet chocolate, chopped

3/4 cup sweet butter, cut into pieces

2 teaspoons vanilla extract

5 eggs, separated

generous 1/4 cup flour, sifted

pinch of salt

confectioner's sugar, for dusting

whipped cream sweetened with confectioner's sugar, to serve

Preheat the oven to 325°F. Generously grease a 9½-inch springform cake pan. Sprinkle with a little sugar and tap out the excess.

Set aside 3 tablespoons of the sugar. Place the chocolate, butter, and remaining sugar in a large heavy-based pan and cook over a moderate heat until the chocolate and butter have melted and the sugar has dissolved. Remove the pan from the heat, stir in the vanilla extract and let the mixture cool slightly.

Beat the egg yolks into the chocolate mixture, beating well after each addition, then stir in the flour. In a large bowl, scrupulously clean and grease-free, and using clean beaters, whisk the egg whites, adding the salt, until they will hold stiff peaks. Alternatively use an electric mixer. Sprinkle over the reserved sugar and beat until the whites are stiff and glossy. Beat one-third of the egg whites into the chocolate mixture, then carefully fold in the remaining whites.

Carefully pour the mixture into the prepared pan and tap the pan gently to release any air bubbles.

Bake the cake for about 35–45 minutes until well risen or until a skewer inserted into the center comes out clean. (If the cake appears to rise unevenly, rotate after 20–25 minutes.) Transfer the cake to a wire rack, remove the side of the pan and let cool completely. Remove the pan base. Dust the cake

with confectioner's sugar and transfer to a serving plate. Serve with the whipped cream.

DEATH BY CHOCOLATE

There are many versions of this cake; this is a very rich one which is ideal for a large party.

Serves 18–20

8 ounces bittersweet chocolate

½ cup sweet butter, cut into pieces

⅔ cup water

generous 1 cup granulated sugar

2 teaspoons vanilla extract

2 eggs, separated

⅔ cup buttermilk

generous 3 cups flour

2 teaspoons baking powder

1 teaspoon baking soda

pinch of cream of tartar

chocolate curls, raspberries, and
* confectioner's sugar, to decorate*

For the fudge filling

1 pound bittersweet chocolate

1 cup sweet butter

⅓ cup brandy or rum

¾ cup seedless raspberry preserve

For the chocolate ganache glaze

1 cup heavy cream

8 ounces bittersweet chocolate

2 tablespoons brandy

Preheat the oven to 350°F. Grease and base-line a 10-inch spring-form cake pan. Place the chocolate, chopped, butter, and water in a pan. Cook over moderate heat until melted. Remove from heat, beat in the sugar and vanilla and cool. Beat the egg yolks and then stir in the chocolate mixture. Gently fold in the buttermilk. Sift the flour, baking powder, and soda into a bowl, then fold into the chocolate mixture. Whisk the egg whites and cream of tartar until they peak stiffly. Fold in the chocolate mixture. Pour the mixture into the pan. Bake for 45–50 minutes. Cool for 10 minutes on a wire rack. Run a knife around the edge of the pan. Remove the side. Invert cake on to wire rack, remove the base of pan and cool. Wash the pan.

For the filling, melt the chocolate, butter, and 4 tablespoons brandy or rum over moderate heat, stirring. Set aside to thicken. Cut the cake cross-ways into three. Melt the raspberry preserve and remaining brandy or rum, stirring. Spread thinly over each cake layer. Allow to set. Place the base cake layer back in the pan. Spread with half the filling, top with the second cake layer, spread with the remaining filling and top with the top cake layer, preserve side down. Press the layers together, cover, and chill for 4–6 hours. Run a knife around the edge of the cake to loosen, unclip and remove side of pan. Set the cake on a wire rack over a baking sheet.

Bring the cream to a boil. Remove from heat, add the chocolate, chopped, stirring until melted. Stir in the brandy and strain into a bowl. Stand for 4–5 minutes to thicken. Working out toward the edge of the bowl, whisk the glaze until shiny. Pour over the cake using a metal spatula to smooth the top and sides; allow to set. Slide the cake on to a serving plate. Decorate with chocolate curls and raspberries. Dust with confectioner's sugar.

CHOCOLATE AND ORANGE ANGEL CAKE

This light-as-air sponge with its fluffy icing is virtually fat-free, yet tastes heavenly.

Serves 10
¼ cup flour
2 tablespoons unsweetened cocoa powder
2 tablespoons cornstarch
pinch of salt
5 egg whites
½ teaspoon cream of tartar
½ cup superfine sugar
blanched and shredded rind of
* 1 orange, to decorate*

For the icing
scant 1 cup superfine sugar
1 egg white

Preheat the oven to 350°F. Sift the flour, cocoa powder, cornstarch, and salt together three times. In a large bowl, clean and grease-free, whisk the egg whites until foamy. Add the cream of tartar, then whisk again until soft peaks form.

Gradually add the superfine sugar to the egg whites a spoonful at a time, whisking after each addition. Sift a third of the flour and cocoa mixture over the meringue and gently fold in. Repeat, sifting and folding in the flour and cocoa mixture two more times.

Spoon the mixture into a nonstick 8-inch ring mold and level the top. Bake in the oven for 35 minutes or until springy when lightly pressed. Turn upside-down on to a wire cooling rack. Allow to cool in the mold. Carefully ease out of the mold.

To make the icing, put the superfine sugar in a pan with 5 tablespoons cold water. Stir over low heat until dissolved. Boil this syrup until it reaches a temperature of 250°F on a sugar thermometer, or when a drop of the syrup makes a soft ball when dropped into a cup of cold water. Remove from the heat immediately.

Whisk the egg white until it is stiff. Add the sugar syrup in a thin stream, whisking all the time. Continue to whisk until the icing mixture is very thick and fluffy.

Spread the icing over the top and sides of the cooled cake. Sprinkle the orange rind over the top of the cake and serve.

COOK'S TIP
Make sure you do not overbeat the egg whites. They should not be stiff but should form soft peaks, so that the air bubbles can expand during cooking and help the cake to rise.

CHOCOLATE NUT CAKE

There is a choice of nuts to use in this cake according to your preference.

Serves 6–8

unsweetened cocoa powder, for dusting

6 ounces semisweet chocolate, chopped
  into small pieces

4 ounces sweet butter

1 cup superfine sugar

4 eggs, separated

1 cup freshly ground unsalted
  macadamia nuts or almonds

¼ cup flour

pinch of cream of tartar (optional)

whipped cream sweetened with
  confectioner's sugar, to serve

COOK'S TIP

*Beating egg whites should
always be the last step in
preparation of cakes or any other
recipes. Once they are beaten,
they should be folded in at once,
not left to stand.*

Preheat the oven to 325°F. Grease and line a 9-inch round cake pan. Dust the pan with cocoa powder.

Put the chocolate and butter in a heavy-based pan. Stir until melted. Let cool. Beat together the sugar and egg yolks until pale and thick. Add the chocolate mixture, nuts, and flour and beat in gently.

In a large bowl, clean and grease-free, beat the egg whites until they peak stiffly. (If not using a copper bowl, add the cream of tartar when the whites are frothy.) Add about one-quarter of the whites to the chocolate mixture and mix in gently using a rubber spatula. It is not necessary to blend thoroughly. Add the remaining egg whites and fold them in gently but thoroughly.

Pour the batter into the prepared pan. Bake until a skewer inserted into the center of the cake comes out clean, 1–1¼ hours.

Cool in the pan for 10 minutes, then turn out on to a wire rack to cool completely. Dust with cocoa powder and serve with whipped cream.

CHOCOLATE TRUFFLES

These truffles, like the prized fungi they resemble, are a Christmas specialty in France.

Makes 20–30

¾ cup heavy cream

10 ounces semisweet chocolate, chopped

2 tablespoons sweet butter, cut into pieces

2–3 tablespoons brandy (optional)

For the coatings

unsweetened cocoa powder

finely chopped pistachios or hazelnuts

14 ounces semisweet, milk, or white chocolate, or a mixture

Place the cream in a pan and bring to a boil over a moderate heat. Remove from the heat and add the chocolate, stirring until melted. Stir in the butter and the brandy, if using, then strain into a bowl and let cool. Cover and chill for 6–8 hours. Line a baking sheet with wax paper. Using two teaspoons, form the mixture into 20–30 balls and place on the paper. Chill to harden.

To coat the truffles, sift the cocoa powder into a small bowl, drop in one truffle at a time, and roll to coat well. Roll some truffles in finely chopped pistachios or hazelnuts and freeze for 1 hour. To coat with chocolate, melt the semisweet, milk, or white chocolate in a bowl over a pan of simmering water, stirring until melted, then allow to cool slightly. Using a fork, dip one truffle at a time into the chocolate, tapping the fork on the bowl edge to shake off the excess. Place the truffles on a baking sheet lined with baking parchment and chill at once. If the chocolate thickens, reheat until smooth. Chill, well wrapped, for up to ten days.

CHOCOLATE CHEESECAKE

A luscious cheesecake prettily decorated using a paper doily.

Serves 12

1 pound semisweet chocolate, broken
   into pieces
1/2 cup superfine sugar
2 teaspoons vanilla extract
4 eggs
3 × 8-ounce packages cream cheese, at
   room temperature
2–3 tablespoons confectioner's sugar,
   to decorate

For the crust

1 cup graham cracker crumbs
5 tablespoons butter or
   margarine, melted
2 tablespoons grated
   semisweet chocolate
2 tablespoons superfine sugar

COOK'S TIP

For an all-chocolate cheesecake,
use finely crushed chocolate
wafers for the crust.

Preheat the oven to 325°F. Lightly grease and base-line a 9- or 10-inch springform cake pan.

To make the crust, mix together the graham cracker crumbs, melted butter or margarine, grated chocolate, and sugar until thoroughly combined. Pat evenly over the bottom and up the sides of the prepared pan. (The crust is intended to be thin.)

In a heatproof bowl set over a pan of barely simmering water, or in a double-boiler, melt the chocolate with the superfine sugar. Remove the bowl from the heat and stir in the vanilla extract. Set aside and allow the mixture to cool briefly.

In another bowl, beat together the eggs and cream cheese until smooth and homogeneous. Gently stir in the cooled chocolate mixture until it is completely blended.

Pour the chocolate filling into the crumb crust. Bake for about 45 minutes or until the filling is set. Allow to cool, in the pan, on a wire cooling rack. Chill for at least 12 hours.

Transfer the cheesecake to a serving plate and remove the side of the pan. To decorate, lay a paper doily on the surface of the cake and sift the confectioner's sugar evenly over the doily. With two hands, carefully lift off the doily to reveal the pattern.

CHOCOLATE CHESTNUT ROULADE

The candied chestnuts could be dipped in melted semisweet chocolate for the decoration.

Serves 10–12

6 ounces bittersweet chocolate, chopped
2 tablespoons unsweetened cocoa
   powder, sifted
¼ cup strong coffee or espresso
6 eggs, separated
6 tablespoons superfine sugar
pinch of cream of tartar
1 teaspoon vanilla extract
unsweetened cocoa powder, for dusting
candied chestnuts, to decorate

For the chestnut cream filling
2 cups heavy cream
2 tablespoons rum or coffee-
   flavor liqueur
1½ cups canned sweetened
   chestnut purée
4 ounces bittersweet chocolate, grated

Preheat the oven to 350°F. Grease and line the bottom and sides of a 15½ × 10½ × 1-inch jelly roll pan, allowing a 1-inch overhang. In a heat-proof bowl set over a pan of simmering water, melt the chocolate until smooth. Set aside. Dissolve the cocoa in the coffee to make a smooth paste. Set aside.

In a mixing bowl with an electric mixer, beat the egg yolks with half the sugar until pale and thick, about 3–5 minutes. Slowly beat in the melted chocolate and cocoa-coffee paste until just blended.

Beat the egg whites and cream of tartar until stiff peaks form. Sprinkle the sugar over the whites in two batches and beat until whites are stiff and glossy; beat in the vanilla. Stir a spoonful of whites into the chocolate mixture to lighten it, then fold in the remaining whites. Spoon into the pan. Bake for 20 to 25 minutes or until the cake springs back when touched with a fingertip.

Meanwhile, dust a dish towel with cocoa powder. When the cake is done, turn out on to the towel immediately and remove paper. Starting at a narrow end, roll cake and towel together jelly roll style. Cool completely.

To make the filling, whip the cream and rum or liqueur until soft peaks form. Beat a spoonful of cream into the chestnut purée to lighten it, then fold in the remaining cream and grated chocolate. Reserve a quarter of the chestnut cream mixture for the decoration.

Unroll the roulade and trim the edges. Spread the chestnut cream mixture to within 1 inch of the edge of the cake. Using the towel to lift the cake, gently re-roll the cake. Place roulade seam-side down on a serving plate. Spread the reserved chestnut cream over the top of the roulade, and spoon some into an icing bag fitted with a medium star tip. Pipe rosettes down the sides and decorate with candied chestnuts.

RICH CHOCOLATE CAKE

This dark, fudgy cake is easy to make, stores well, and is a chocolate lover's dream come true.

Serves 14–16

1 cup sweet butter, cut into pieces

9 ounces semisweet chocolate, chopped

5 eggs

½ cup superfine sugar, plus

*   1 tablespoon and extra for sprinkling*

1 tablespoon cocoa powder

2 teaspoons vanilla extract

unsweetened cocoa powder, for dusting

chocolate shavings, to decorate

Preheat the oven to 325°F. Lightly grease and base-line a 9-inch spring-form cake pan. Butter the paper and sprinkle with a little sugar, then tap out the excess sugar from the pan.

The cake is baked in a *bain-marie*, so carefully wrap the base and sides of the pan with a double thickness of foil to prevent water leaking into the cake.

In a heatproof bowl set over a pan of barely simmering water, or in a double-boiler, melt the butter and chocolate. Beat the eggs with 7 tablespoons of the sugar using an electric mixer.

Mix together the cocoa powder and 1 tablespoon sugar and beat into the egg mixture until well blended. Beat in the vanilla extract, then slowly beat in the melted chocolate until well blended. Pour the mixture into the prepared pan and tap gently to release any air bubbles.

Place the cake pan in a roasting pan and pour in boiling water to come ¾ inch up the side of the wrapped pan. Bake for 45–50 minutes or until the edge of the cake is set and the center still soft (a skewer inserted 2 inches from the edge should come out clean). Lift the pan out of the water and remove the foil. Transfer to a wire cooling rack, remove the side of the pan and let the cake cool completely (the cake will sink a little in the center).

Invert the cake on to the wire rack. Remove the base of the pan and the paper. Dust the cake liberally with cocoa powder and arrange the chocolate shavings around the edge. Slide the cake on to a serving plate.

Pies and Pastries

Rich chocolate pastry combines with velvety smooth

creamy chocolate, gleaming berries and crunchy

nut fillings, in luxuriously luscious pies,

tarts and cream puffs.

VELVET MOCHA CREAM PIE

The texture of this pie is as smooth and rich as velvet.

Serves 8

2 teaspoons instant espresso coffee

2 tablespoons hot water

6 ounces semisweet chocolate

1 ounce square bittersweet chocolate

1½ cups whipping cream

½ cup whipped cream and chocolate-
coated coffee beans, to decorate

For the crust

1½ cups chocolate wafer crumbs

2 tablespoons sugar

⅓ cup butter, melted

For the crust, mix the chocolate wafer crumbs and sugar together, then stir in the melted butter. Press the crumbs evenly over the base and side of a 9-inch pie pan. Chill until firm. In a bowl, dissolve the coffee in the water and set aside. Melt both the chocolates in a heatproof bowl set over a pan of hot water. Remove from the heat when nearly melted and stir to continue melting. Set the base of the pan in cool water to reduce the temperature. Be careful not to splash any water on the chocolate. Pour the cream into a mixing bowl set in hot water to warm it.

Whip the cream until light and fluffy. Add the dissolved coffee and whip until the cream just holds its shape. When the chocolate is at room temperature, fold it gently into the cream. Pour into the chilled crumb crust and chill until firm. To serve, pipe a ring of whipped cream rosettes around the edge, then place the coffee beans in the center of each.

CHOCOLATE CHIP PECAN PIE

A handsome pie suitable for an elegant dinner party dessert.

Serves 8–10
1½ cups flour
1 tablespoon superfine sugar
½ teaspoon salt
½ cup unsalted butter, cut into
  small pieces
½ cup iced water

For the filling
3 ounces unsweetened
  chocolate, chopped
4 tablespoons butter, cut into pieces
3 eggs
scant ¾ cup light or dark
  brown sugar
¾ cup corn syrup
1 tablespoon vanilla extract
2 cups pecan halves
½ cup plain chocolate chips

To make the pastry, blend the flour, sugar, and salt in a food processor or blender. Add the butter and process for 15–20 seconds until the mixture resembles coarse crumbs. With machine running, add iced water, until the dough begins to stick together; do not allow it to form a ball or pastry will be tough. Shape into a flat disc and wrap tightly in waxed paper. Chill for 1 hour. Butter a 9-inch tart pan. Soften the dough for 10–15 minutes at room temperature. On a floured surface, roll out the dough into a 12-inch round, ⅛ inch thick. Use to line the tart pan. Trim the pastry even with the rim of the pie pan; using fingers, flatten to rim of pie pan. Re-roll trimmings to a long rectangle and cut thin strips about ¼ inch wide. Braid three strips together. Repeat until you have enough to fit around the pie edge. Brush the pastry edge with water and press on the braids. Prick the base with a fork. Chill for 30 minutes.

Preheat the oven to 400°F. Line the pastry shell with wax paper and fill with dry beans. Bake for 5 minutes, lift out the paper and beans and bake for 5 minutes more. Remove to a wire rack to cool slightly. Lower the oven temperature to 375°F.

For the filling, melt the chocolate and butter in a pan over low heat, stirring until smooth. Set aside to cool slightly. Beat the eggs with the sugar, syrup, and vanilla in a bowl. Slowly beat in the melted chocolate. Arrange the pecan halves and the chocolate chips over the base of the pastry. Place the pie pan on a baking sheet and carefully pour the chocolate mixture into the shell. Bake for 35–45 minutes, until the chocolate mixture is set. If the pastry edge begins to brown too quickly, cover with strips of foil. Remove the pie to a wire rack to cool. Serve warm or chilled.

RICH CHOCOLATE-BERRY TART

Raspberries, blackberries, alpine strawberries, boysenberries, or loganberries may be used in this tart.

Serves 10

½ cup sweet butter, softened

½ cup superfine sugar

½ teaspoon salt

1 tablespoon vanilla extract

½ cup unsweetened cocoa powder

1½ cups flour

1 pound fresh berries, for topping

For the ganache filling

2 cups heavy cream

*½ cup seedless blackberry or
    raspberry preserve*

8 ounces bittersweet chocolate, chopped

*2 tablespoons unsalted butter, cut
    into pieces*

For the sauce

*8 ounces fresh or frozen blackberries
    or raspberries, thawed*

1 tablespoon lemon juice

2 tablespoons superfine sugar

*2 tablespoons blackberry, or raspberry-
    flavor liqueur*

To make the pastry, process the butter, sugar, salt, and vanilla in a food processor or blender until creamy. Add the cocoa and process for 1 minute; scrape the side of the bowl. Add the flour all at once and using the pulse action, process for 10–15 seconds, until just blended. Put a piece of plastic wrap on the work surface and turn out the dough on to it. Use the wrap to help shape the dough into a flat disc. Wrap tightly and chill for 1 hour.

Grease a 9-inch tart pan with removable base. Soften the dough for 10 minutes at room temperature. Roll it out between two sheets of plastic wrap to an 11-inch round, ¼ inch thick. Peel off the top sheet of plastic and invert the dough into the pan. Ease it in and remove the plastic wrap.

With floured fingers, press the dough on to the base and side of the pan, trim off any excess dough and prick the base with a fork. Chill for 1 hour. Preheat oven to 350°F. Line the tart shell with baking parchment and fill with dry beans. Bake for 10 minutes. Lift out paper and beans and bake for 5 minutes more. Remove to a wire rack to cool completely.

To make the filling, bring the cream and preserve to a boil in a pan over a moderate heat. Remove from the heat and add the chocolate all at once, stirring until melted and smooth. Stir in the butter and strain into the tart shell, smoothing the top. Cool the tart completely.

To make the sauce, combine the berries, lemon juice, and sugar in a food processor and process until smooth. Strain into a small bowl and add the liqueur. If the sauce is too thick, thin with a little water.

Remove the tart from the pan. Place on a serving plate and arrange the berries on the top of the tart. With a pastry brush, brush the berries with a little of the berry sauce to glaze. Serve the remaining sauce separately.

CHOCOLATE APRICOT LINZER TART

To create a striped effect, place wax paper strips on the tart before dusting with confectioner's sugar.

Serves 10–12

generous ¹/₂ cup whole blanched
  almonds
¹/₂ cup superfine sugar
generous 1¹/₂ cups flour
2 tablespoons unsweetened
  cocoa powder
1 teaspoon ground cinnamon
¹/₂ teaspoon salt
1 teaspoon grated orange rind
1 cup sweet butter, cut into pieces
2–3 tablespoons iced water
¹/₂ cup semisweet chocolate chips
confectioner's sugar, for dusting

For the apricot filling

12 ounces ready-to-eat dried apricots
¹/₂ cup orange juice
³/₄ cup water
3 tablespoons granulated sugar
2 tablespoons apricot preserve
¹/₂ teaspoon ground cinnamon
¹/₂ teaspoon almond extract

To make the filling, bring the apricots, orange juice, and water to a boil over moderate heat. Lower the heat and simmer for 15–20 minutes until the liquid is absorbed, stirring frequently. Stir in the sugar, apricot preserve, cinnamon, and almond extract. Press the mixture through a strainer into a bowl, cool, then cover and chill.

To make the pastry, butter an 11-inch tart pan with removable base. In a food processor or blender, finely grind the almonds with half the sugar. Sift the flour, cocoa, remaining sugar, cinnamon, and salt into a bowl. Add to the food processor and blend. Add the orange rind and butter and process for 20 seconds more. Add 2 tablespoons iced water and using pulse action, process until dough just begins to stick together. If it appears too dry, add more iced water, little by little, until it holds together.

Knead the dough until just blended. Divide in half. Press half the dough onto the base and side of pan. Prick base with a fork. Chill for 30 minutes. Roll out remaining dough between two sheets of plastic wrap to an 11-inch round. Slide it on to a baking sheet and chill for 30 minutes.

Preheat the oven to 350°F. Spread the filling on to the base. Sprinkle with chocolate chips. Set aside. Slide the dough round on to a floured surface and cut into ¹/₂-inch wide strips; allow to soften for 3–5 minutes.

Place half the strips ¹/₂ inch apart over the filling. Place the remaining strips diagonally across the bottom strips. Press down on each side of each crossing to accentuate the lattice effect. Press ends to side of tart and trim.

Bake for 35–40 minutes until the top of the pastry is set and the filling bubbles. Cool on a wire rack to room temperature. To serve, remove side of pan and dust confectioner's sugar over the top pastry strips.

CHOCOLATE CREAM PUFFS

This mouth-watering dessert is served in cafés throughout France. Sometimes the cream puffs are filled with whipped cream instead of ice cream, but they are always drizzled with chocolate sauce.

Serves 4–6

10 ounces semisweet chocolate

1/2 cup warm water

3 cups vanilla ice cream

For the cream puffs

3/4 cup flour

1/4 teaspoon salt

pinch of ground nutmeg

3/4 cup water

6 tablespoons sweet butter, cut into 6 pieces

3 eggs

Preheat the oven to 400°F and lightly grease a large baking sheet. To make the cream puffs, sift together the flour, salt, and nutmeg. In a pan, bring the water and butter to a boil. Remove from the heat and add the dry ingredients all at once. Beat with a wooden spoon for about 1 minute until well blended and the mixture starts to pull away from the sides of the pan. Then set the pan over low heat and cook the mixture for about 2 minutes, beating constantly. Remove from the heat.

Beat one egg in a small bowl and set aside. Add the remaining eggs, one at a time, to the flour mixture, beating well after each addition. Add the beaten egg by teaspoonfuls until the dough is smooth and shiny; it should pull away and fall slowly when dropped from a spoon.

Using a tablespoon, drop the dough on to the baking sheet in 12 mounds. Bake for 25–30 minutes until the pastry is well risen and browned. Turn off the oven and leave the puffs to cool with the oven door open.

To make the sauce, place the chocolate and water in a double-boiler or in a bowl placed over a pan of hot water and let melt, stirring occasionally. Keep warm until ready to serve, or reheat, over simmering water.

Split the cream puffs in half and put a small scoop of ice cream in each. Arrange on a serving platter or divide among individual plates. Pour the chocolate sauce over the top and serve at once.

Cookies and Bakes

Crisp and crunchy cookies, simply gorgeous gooey

brownies, fabulous fruity muffins, and rich gingery

florentines are mouth-watering chocolaty treats – totally

irresistible and satisfying at any time of day.

CHOCOLATE FUDGE BROWNIES

The ultimate tea-time treat, brownies are a firm family favorite.

Makes 12

3/4 cup butter

generous 1/2 cup unsweetened
   cocoa powder

2 eggs, lightly beaten

3/4 cup brown sugar

1/2 teaspoon vanilla extract

1 cup chopped pecans

1/2 cup self-rising flour

For the frosting

4 ounces semisweet chocolate

2 tablespoons butter

1 tablespoon sour cream

Preheat the oven to 350°F. Grease and base-line an 8-inch square, shallow cake pan. Melt the butter in a pan and stir in the cocoa powder.

Beat together the eggs, sugar, and vanilla extract in a bowl, then stir in the cooled cocoa mixture with the nuts. Sift over the flour and fold in.

Pour the mixture into the prepared pan and bake for 30–35 minutes, until risen. Remove from the oven (the mixture will still be quite soft and wet, but it cooks further while cooling) and leave to cool in the pan.

To make the frosting, melt the chocolate and butter together in a pan and remove from the heat. Beat in the sour cream until smooth and glossy. Let cool slightly and then spread over the top of the brownies. When the frosting is set, cut into 12 pieces.

CHEWY CHOCOLATE COOKIES

Make two batches of these cookies at a time – they will disappear very quickly!

Makes 18

4 egg whites

2¹/₂ cups confectioner's sugar

1 cup unsweetened cocoa powder

2 tablespoons flour

1 teaspoon instant coffee powder

1 tablespoon water

1 cup walnuts, finely chopped

Preheat the oven to 350°F. Line two baking sheets with wax paper and grease the paper.

Beat the egg whites until frothy with an electric mixer. Sift the sugar, cocoa powder, flour, and coffee into the whites. Add the water and continue beating on low speed to blend, then on high for a few minutes until the mixture thickens. With a rubber spatula, fold in the walnuts.

Place generous tablespoonfuls of the mixture 1 inch apart on the prepared sheets. Bake for 12–15 minutes until firm and cracked on top but soft on the inside. Using a metal spatula, transfer to a wire rack to cool.

COOK'S TIP
If wished, add ¹/₂ cup chocolate chips to the cookie dough along with the nuts.

CHOCOLATE BLUEBERRY MUFFINS

Paper liners not only make for easier washing up, but they also keep the muffins fresher.

Makes 12

½ cup butter

*3 ounces unsweetened
  chocolate, chopped*

1 cup granulated sugar

1 egg, lightly beaten

1 cup buttermilk

2 teaspoons vanilla extract

2 cups flour

1 teaspoon baking soda

*1 cup fresh or frozen
  blueberries, thawed*

1 ounce bittersweet chocolate, melted

Preheat the oven to 375°F. Melt the butter and chocolate in a pan over moderate heat until smooth, stirring frequently. Remove from the heat to cool slightly.

Stir in the sugar, egg, buttermilk, and vanilla extract. Gently fold in the flour and baking soda until just blended. (Do not overblend; the mixture may be lumpy with some unblended flour.) Fold in the berries.

Spoon the mixture into twelve greased or paper-lined 2½-inch muffin cups, filling to the top. Bake for 25–30 minutes until a skewer inserted in the center comes out with just a few crumbs attached. Remove the muffins in their paper liners to a wire cooling rack immediately (if left in the pan they will go soggy). Drizzle with the melted chocolate and serve warm or cool.

Black and White Ginger Florentines

These delicious florentines can be stored in an airtight container in the fridge for up to one week.

Makes about 30

½ cup heavy cream

¼ cup sweet butter

7 tablespoons granulated sugar

2 tablespoons honey

1¼ cups slivered almonds

⅓ cup flour

½ teaspoon ground ginger

⅓ cup diced candied orange peel

½ cup diced preserved ginger

2 ounces semisweet chocolate, chopped

5 ounces bittersweet chocolate, chopped

5 ounces white chocolate, chopped

Preheat the oven to 350°F. Lightly grease two large baking sheets. (Nonstick sheets are ideal for these caramel-like cookies.) Stir the cream, butter, sugar, and honey in a pan over a moderate heat until the sugar dissolves. Bring the mixture to a boil, stirring constantly. Remove from the heat and stir in the almonds, flour, and ground ginger until well blended. Stir in the orange peel, stem ginger, and chopped semisweet chocolate.

Drop teaspoonfuls of mixture on to prepared sheets at least 3 inches apart. Spread each round as thinly as possible with the back of the spoon.

Bake for 8–10 minutes or until the edges are golden brown and the cookies are bubbling. Do not underbake or they will be sticky, but be careful not to overbake as the high sugar and fat content allows them to burn easily. Continue baking in batches. If you wish, use a 3-inch cookie cutter to neaten the edges of the florentines while on the baking sheets. Remove the baking sheet to a wire cooling rack for 10 minutes. Then, with a metal spatula, remove the cookies to a wire rack to cool completely.

In a small pan over a very low heat, heat the bittersweet chocolate, stirring frequently, until melted and smooth. Cool slightly. In a heatproof bowl set over a pan of simmering water or in a double-boiler, melt the white chocolate until smooth, stirring frequently. Remove top of double-boiler from base and cool for about 5 minutes, stirring occasionally until slightly thickened.

Using a small, metal spatula, spread half the florentines with the bittersweet chocolate on the flat side of each cookie, swirling to create a decorative surface, and place on a wire rack, chocolate side up. Spread remaining florentines with the melted white chocolate and place on rack, chocolate side up. Chill for 10–15 minutes to set completely.

Hot Desserts

Rich and dark, creamy white, and simple milk chocolate

make delicious desserts, sensational soufflés, a wonderful

hot chocolate cake and an almondy peach pudding

that is sheer indulgence.

CHOCOLATE AMARETTI PEACHES

Quick and easy to prepare, this delicious dessert can also be made with fresh nectarines or apricots.

Serves 4

4 ounces amaretti cookies, crushed

2 ounces semisweet chocolate, chopped

grated rind of 1/2 orange

1 tablespoon clear honey

1/4 teaspoon ground cinnamon

1 egg white, lightly beaten

4 firm, ripe peaches

2/3 cup white wine

1 tablespoon superfine sugar

whipped cream, to serve

Preheat the oven to 375°F. Mix together the crushed amaretti cookies, chocolate, orange rind, honey, and cinnamon in a bowl. Add the beaten egg white and stir to bind the mixture together.

Halve and pit the peaches and fill the cavities with the chocolate mixture, mounding it up slightly.

Arrange the stuffed peaches in a lightly buttered, shallow ovenproof dish which will just hold the fruit comfortably. Pour the wine into a measuring cup and stir in the sugar.

Pour the wine mixture around the peaches. Bake for 30–40 minutes, until the peaches are tender. Serve at once with a little of the cooking juices spooned over and the whipped cream.

HOT CHOCOLATE CAKE

This is wonderfully wicked, either hot served with a white chocolate sauce, or cold. The basic cake freezes well – thaw, then warm in the microwave before serving.

Makes 10–12 slices

generous 1¾ cups self-rising whole
   wheat flour
¼ cup unsweetened cocoa powder
pinch of salt
¾ cup soft margarine
¾ cup brown sugar
few drops of vanilla extract
4 eggs
3 ounces white chocolate,
   roughly chopped
chocolate leaves and curls, to decorate

For the white chocolate sauce

3 ounces white chocolate
⅔ cup light cream
2–3 tablespoons milk

Preheat the oven to 325°F. Sift the flour, cocoa powder, and salt into a bowl, adding back in the whole wheat flakes from the sifter.

In another bowl, cream the margarine, sugar, and vanilla extract together until light and fluffy, then gently beat in one egg.

Gradually stir in the remaining eggs, one at a time, alternately folding in some of the flour. Then add the remaining flour and stir until all the flour mixture is blended in well.

Stir in the white chocolate and spoon into a 1½–2-pound loaf pan or a greased 7-inch cake pan. Bake for 30–40 minutes, or until just firm to the touch and shrinking away from the sides of the pan.

To make the sauce, heat the chocolate and cream very gently in a pan until the chocolate is melted. Remove from the heat. Gradually add the milk and stir until cool.

Serve the cake in generous slices, in a pool of sauce and decorated with chocolate leaves and curls.

HOT MOCHA SOUFFLES

These hot, sweet soufflés are easy to make, but don't be tempted to open the oven door during cooking!

Serves 4

4 tablespoons butter

⅓ cup flour

1¼ cups milk

4 ounces semisweet chocolate,
  finely chopped

1 tablespoon instant coffee granules

6 tablespoons superfine sugar, plus
  extra for coating the dishes

5 eggs, separated

confectioner's sugar, for dusting

Preheat the oven to 375°F, then generously butter four 1¼-cup soufflé dishes, especially around the rims.

Sprinkle the dishes heavily with sugar and set aside. Melt the butter in a heavy-based pan. Stir in the flour and cook for 1 minute. Gradually add the milk and cook, stirring until thickened. Cook for 1–2 minutes, stirring.

Remove the pan from the heat and beat in the chocolate and coffee. Cool the chocolate mixture slightly, then beat in the sugar and egg yolks. Whisk the egg whites until stiff. Add a tablespoonful to the chocolate sauce and beat in to lighten the mixture. Gently fold in the rest.

Spoon the mixture into the dishes and bake for 20 minutes, or until well risen and just firm to the touch. Dust with confectioner's sugar and serve.

CHOCOLATE, DATE, AND WALNUT DESSERT

Sticky dates and crunchy walnuts make this a dessert of wonderful contrasts.

Serves 4

4 tablespoons chopped walnuts

2 tablespoons chopped dates

2 eggs

1 teaspoon vanilla extract

2 tablespoons raw sugar

3 tablespoons whole wheat flour

1 tablespoon unsweetened cocoa powder

2 tablespoons milk

Preheat the oven to 350°F. Grease a 5-cup pudding mold and place a small circle of wax or baking parchment in the base. Mix the walnuts and dates together and then spoon into the pudding mold.

Separate the eggs and place the yolks in a bowl, with the vanilla and sugar. Place over a pan of hot water and whisk until the mixture is thick and pale.

Sift the flour and cocoa powder into the mixture and fold them in with a metal spoon. Stir in the milk, to soften the mixture slightly. Whisk the egg whites until they hold soft peaks and fold them in.

Spoon the mixture into the mold and bake for 40–45 minutes, or until the pudding is well risen and firm to the touch. Run a knife around the pudding to loosen it from the mold, and then turn it out and serve immediately.

Cold Desserts

Aromatic vanilla, coffee and spicy ginger make perfect

partners in delectable chilled chocolate desserts,

irresistible ice creams, marvelous marquises, creamy

custards and melt-in-the-mouth mousses and timbales.

MOCHA CREAM POTS

The addition of coffee to this classic French dessert gives it an exotic touch.

Serves 8

1 tablespoon instant coffee powder

2 cups milk

6 tablespoons superfine sugar

8 ounces semisweet chocolate, chopped

2 teaspoons vanilla extract

2 tablespoons coffee liqueur (optional)

7 egg yolks

whipped cream and candied cake

  decorations, to decorate

Preheat the oven to 325°F. Place eight ½-cup dessert cups or ramekins in a roasting pan.

Put the instant coffee into a pan and stir in the milk, then add the sugar and set the pan over a medium-high heat. Bring to a boil, stirring constantly, until the coffee and sugar have dissolved. Remove the pan from the heat and add the chocolate. Stir until smooth. Stir in the vanilla extract and coffee liqueur, if using.

Whisk the egg yolks lightly in a bowl. Slowly whisk in the chocolate mixture until blended, then strain into a large pitcher and divide equally among the cups or ramekins. Pour boiling water into the roasting pan to come halfway up the sides of the cups or ramekins.

Bake for about 30–35 minutes or until the custard is just set and a knife inserted into a custard comes out clean. Remove the cups or ramekins from the roasting pan and allow to cool. Place on a baking sheet, cover and chill completely. Decorate with whipped cream and candied cake decorations.

CHILLED CHOCOLATE PIE

This is a very rich family dessert, but it is also designed to use up the occasional leftover! You don't need to eat it in a rush – it keeps very well.

Serves 6–8

½ cup butter, melted

8 ounces ginger cookies, finely crushed

1 cup stale spongecake crumbs

4–5 tablespoons orange juice

½ cup pitted dates, warmed

¼ cup finely chopped nuts

6 ounces bittersweet chocolate

1¼ cups whipping cream

grated chocolate and confectioner's sugar, to serve

Mix together the butter and ginger cookie crumbs, then pack around the base and side of a 7-inch loose-based pie pan. Chill.

Put the cake crumbs into a large bowl with the orange juice and let soak. Mash the warm dates thoroughly and blend into the cake crumbs along with the nuts.

Melt the chocolate with 3–4 tablespoons of the cream. Softly whip the rest of the cream, then fold in the melted chocolate.

Stir the cream and chocolate mixture into the crumbs and mix. Pour into the cookie crust shell, mark into portions and let set. Sprinkle over the grated chocolate and dust with confectioner's sugar. Serve cut in wedges.

CHOCOLATE VANILLA TIMBALES

A light dessert, ideal for serving after a rich main course at a dinner party.

Serves 6

1½ cups milk
2 tablespoons unsweetened cocoa powder
2 eggs
1 teaspoon vanilla extract
3 tablespoons granulated sugar
1 tablespoon powdered gelatin
3 tablespoons hot water
mint sprigs, to decorate

For the sauce

½ cup strained plain yogurt
½ teaspoon vanilla extract
extra cocoa powder, to sprinkle

Place the milk and cocoa powder in a pan and stir until boiling. Separate the eggs and beat the egg yolks with the vanilla and sugar until the mixture is pale and smooth. Pour in the chocolate milk, beating well.

Return the mixture to the pan and stir constantly over gentle heat, without boiling, until it is slightly thickened and smooth. Dissolve the gelatin in the hot water and then quickly stir it into the milk mixture. Let it cool until it is on the verge of setting.

Whisk the egg whites until they hold soft peaks. Fold them quickly into the milk mixture. Spoon the timbale into six molds and chill until set.

To serve, run a knife around the edge, dip the molds quickly into hot water and turn out the chocolate timbales on to serving plates. To make the sauce, stir together the yogurt and vanilla extract and spoon on to the plates. Sift over a little cocoa and decorate each with a mint sprig.

CHOCOLATE LOAF WITH COFFEE SAUCE

This type of chocolate dessert is popular in many French restaurants. Sometimes the loaf is encased
in sponge cake, but this version is easier and it can be served cold or frozen.

Serves 6–8

6 ounces semisweet chocolate, chopped

4 tablespoons butter, softened

4 large eggs, separated

2 tablespoons rum or brandy (optional)

pinch of cream of tartar

chocolate curls and chocolate-coated
* coffee beans, to decorate*

For the coffee sauce

2½ cups milk

9 egg yolks

4 tablespoons superfine sugar

1 teaspoon vanilla extract

1 tablespoon instant coffee powder,
* dissolved in 2 tablespoons hot water*

Line a 5-cup terrine or loaf pan with plastic wrap, being careful to smooth it evenly over the base and sides.

In a heatproof bowl set over a pan of barely simmering water, melt the chocolate for 3–5 minutes, then stir until melted and smooth. Remove the bowl from the pan and quickly beat in the softened butter, egg yolks, one at a time, and rum or brandy, if using.

In a clean, grease-free bowl, use an electric mixer to beat the egg whites slowly until frothy. Add the cream of tartar, increase the speed and continue beating until they form soft peaks, then stiffer peaks that just flop over a little. Stir one-third of the egg whites into the chocolate mixture, then fold in the remaining whites. Pour into the terrine or pan and smooth the top. Cover and freeze until ready to serve.

To make the coffee sauce, bring the milk to a simmer over moderate heat. Whisk the egg yolks and sugar for 2–3 minutes until thick and creamy, then whisk in the hot milk and return the mixture to the saucepan. With a wooden spoon, stir over low heat until the sauce begins to thicken and coat the back of the spoon. Strain the custard into a chilled bowl, then stir in the vanilla extract and dissolved coffee and set aside to cool, stirring occasionally. Chill until ready to serve.

Remove the loaf from the freezer according to whether you want it frozen or just cold. To serve, uncover the terrine or pan and dip the base into hot water for 10 seconds. Invert the dessert on to a board and peel off the plastic wrap. Cut the loaf into slices and serve with the coffee sauce. Decorate with the chocolate curls and chocolate-coated coffee beans.

RIPPLED CHOCOLATE ICE CREAM

Rich, smooth and packed with chocolate, this heavenly ice cream is an all-around-the-world chocoholics' favorite – and it's so easy to make.

Serves 4

4 tablespoons store-bought chocolate
   and hazelnut spread

1⅞ cups heavy cream

1 tablespoon confectioner's sugar, sifted

5 tablespoons chopped semisweet
   chocolate

chocolate curls, to decorate

Mix together the chocolate and hazelnut spread and 5 tablespoons of the heavy cream in a bowl.

Place the remaining cream and the confectioner's sugar in a second bowl and beat until softly whipped. Lightly fold in the chocolate mixture with the chopped chocolate until the mixture is rippled. Transfer to a plastic freezer container and freeze for about 3–4 hours, until firm.

Remove the ice cream from the freezer about 10 minutes before serving to allow it to soften slightly. Spoon or scoop into dessert dishes or glasses and top each serving with a few chocolate curls.

Luxury Mocha Mousse

Chocolate and coffee combine beautifully in this dessert – strictly for the grown-ups.

Serves 6

8 ounces fine quality
*   bittersweet chocolate*
¼ cup espresso or strong coffee
2 tablespoons butter, cut into pieces
2 tablespoons brandy or rum
3 eggs, separated
pinch of salt
3 tablespoons superfine sugar
½ cup whipping cream
2 tablespoons coffee-flavor liqueur
chocolate-coated coffee beans,
*   to decorate*

Melt the chocolate and coffee in a pan, stirring until smooth. Remove from the heat and beat in the butter and brandy or rum.

In a small bowl, beat the yolks lightly then beat into the melted chocolate. Cool. In a large, clean, grease-free bowl, use an electric mixer to beat the whites. Add a pinch of salt and beat on medium speed until soft peaks form. Increase the speed and beat until stiff peaks form. Beat in the sugar, 1 tablespoon at a time, until glossy and stiff. Beat 1 tablespoonful of whites into the chocolate mixture, then fold the chocolate into the remaining whites. Pour into six dishes and chill for 3–4 hours. Beat the cream and liqueur in a bowl until soft peaks form. Spoon into an icing bag and pipe the cream on to the mousses. Decorate each with a chocolate-coated coffee bean.

CHOCOLATE AMARETTO MARQUISE

A 9-inch springform cake pan is ideal for this recipe, but for special occasions it is worth taking extra time to carefully line a heart-shaped pan.

Serves 10–12

1 tablespoon vegetable oil, such as
   peanut or sunflower
7–8 amaretti cookies, finely crushed
2 tablespoons unblanched almonds,
   toasted and finely chopped
1 pound bittersweet or semisweet
   chocolate, broken into pieces
   or chopped
1/3 cup Amaretto liqueur
1/3 cup corn syrup
2 cups heavy cream
unsweetened cocoa powder, for dusting

For the Amaretto cream
1 1/2 cups whipping or heavy cream
2–3 tablespoons Amaretto liqueur

Lightly oil and base-line a 9-inch heart-shaped or springform cake pan, then oil the paper. In a small bowl, combine the crushed amaretti cookies and the chopped almonds. Sprinkle this mixture evenly on to the base of the cake pan.

Place the chocolate, Amaretto liqueur, and corn syrup in a pan over very low heat. Stir frequently until the chocolate is melted and the mixture is smooth. Allow the mixture to cool until it feels just warm to the touch, about 6–8 minutes.

In a bowl with an electric mixer, beat the cream until it just begins to hold its shape. Stir a large spoonful into the chocolate mixture, then quickly add the remaining cream and gently fold into the chocolate mixture. Pour into the prepared pan and tap it gently on the work surface to release any large air bubbles. Cover the pan with plastic wrap and chill overnight.

To unmold, run a thin-bladed, sharp knife under hot water and dry carefully. Run the knife around the edge of the pan to loosen the dessert. Place a serving plate over the pan, then invert to unmold the dessert. Carefully peel off the paper, replacing any crust that sticks to it, and dust with cocoa powder. To serve, whip the cream and Amaretto liqueur until soft peaks form and hand around in a separate bowl.

INDEX

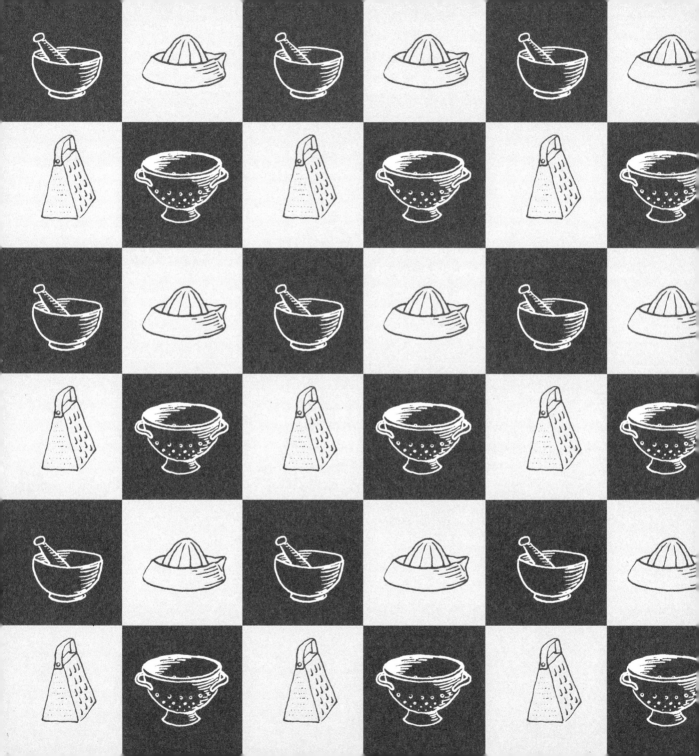